Sniffer dogs and their amazing noses

Most dogs can smell far better than people. They can follow all scents. Sniffer dogs help find lost people. They follow the scent with their noses. Sniffer dogs find people lost in places like ruins and deserts.

A sniffer dog's nose
helps find food in bags
at the city airport.

This dog helps to sniff for weeds and thistles in fields. Then people can dig out the harmful weeds.

Sniffer dogs help to find rare birds. They need to wear a brace on their face or nose. This is so they won't harm the bird when they find it.

brace

Some sniffer dogs smell the scent of pests. A sniffer dog descends into a cellar to race after mice and get them.

Some sniffer dogs hunt for rats in dense bushes. If they find a rat, they bark. This will force the rat out.

Sniffer dogs are let loose to trap a thief. The dogs follow the thief's scent and chase him down.

Some sniffer dogs can
sniff out hidden cash!

Some sniffer dogs can smell the scent of illness. This helps doctors and people with cancer.

Some people like black mushrooms that grow on tree roots. The dogs sniff the tree roots to find the scent. The dog listens to the voice of the farmer, "Go find".

When the dog smells the mushroom, it digs and points to the place with its nose.

Sniffer dogs are smart at
following scents. They have
amazing noses. They help us.

Words to blend

place	city	brace
face	cellar	scent
cancer	force	voice
scents	descends	dense
loose	thistles	listens
race	mice	amazing

Before reading

Synopsis: Most dogs can smell far better than people. Dogs can use their amazing noses to sniff out all sorts of things.

Review phonemes and graphemes: /ear/ ere, eer; /air/ are, ear, ere; /j/ ge, dge, g

Focus phoneme: /s/ **Focus graphemes:** c, ce, sc, se, st

Book discussion: Look at the cover, and read the title together. Talk about sniffer dogs – what do children already know about them? Share their ideas. Ask: *What kind of book do you think this is – fiction or non-fiction? How do you know? What kind of information do you think we will find out about sniffer dogs?*

Link to prior learning: Remind children that the sound /s/ as in 'sit' can also be spelled 'c', 'ce', 'sc', 'se' and 'st'. Turn to page 8 and ask children to find as many words as they can with focus spellings of the /s/ sound (scent, descends, race, mice, cellar).

Vocabulary check: scent: smell – 'They follow the scent with their noses' means 'They follow the smell with their noses'.

Decoding practice: Display the words 'city', 'voice', 'descends', 'dense' and 'thistle'. Can children circle the letter string that makes the /s/ sound, and read each word?

Tricky word practice: Display the word 'have'. Challenge children to circle the tricky part of the word ('ve' which makes the /v/ sound). Practise reading and writing this word.

After reading

Apply learning: Discuss the book. Ask: *What do you think was the most interesting fact about sniffer dogs?*

Comprehension

- How do sniffer dogs find things? (they follow scents with their noses)
- Can sniffer dogs sniff out illness? (yes)
- Where do dogs go to hunt for rats? (dense bushes)

Fluency

- Pick a page that most of the group read quite easily. Ask them to reread it with pace and expression. Model how to do this if necessary.
- Challenge children to read page 2. Encourage them to read clearly and steadily, so that they sound like a TV presenter.
- Practise reading the words on page 17.

Tricky words review

people	the	their
to	are	once
have	into	some
of	laugh	water
friend	school	who